ANIMAL KINGDOM

A Collection of
Rhymed Poems for Kids

BART BILSKI

TOM P. CANNON

DEDICATION

This book is dedicated to all the people who work in wildlife conservation and protect endangered animals. Your hard work and dedication to safeguarding these beautiful creatures will never go unnoticed. Thank you for your tireless efforts and for being the voice of those who cannot speak. You are making a real difference in the world today and for future generations.

CONTENTS

INTRODUCTION

Welcome to The Animal Kingdom! Our collection of rhymed poems for kids celebrates the alluring and enchanting world of animals. Through vivid imagery and fun rhymes, children will learn about the unique physical features, habits, and habitats of twenty different animals, from big cats to elephants to turtles. We hope that this collection will inspire a greater love and appreciation for the creatures that inhabit our planet and give kids a fun and exciting way to learn about the animal kingdom. Enjoy your journey!

Lion

Continent:	Africa
Habitat:	From open plains to thick brush and dry thorn forest.
Life Span:	**Male**: 8-10 years **Female**: 15-16 years
Height:	**Male**: 1.2 m **Female**: 90-110 cm
Weight:	**Male**: 190 kg **Female**: 130 kg
Food Type:	Carnivore
Active Time:	Hunts mostly at night and rests during the day, often active at dawn and dusk and on cooler days
Conservation Status:	Vulnerable
Other:	Speed: 80 km/h

Lions are the king of the land,
Their manes majestic, they take command.
Their roar can be heard from far away,
So, listen up kids, here's what I say.

Lions are the biggest of all cats,
They hunt in groups, and that's a fact.
Their diet is mostly made of meat,
 To find it, they have sharp eyes to seek.

Their manes are full and long and wild,
They look cuddly, but their mood is not mild.
The king of beasts they are indeed,
Living in prides but only one will lead.

Lions are the apex of the food chain,
Their hunting skills are quite plain.
They are a symbol of strength and might,
Their roar and presence are a wondrous sight.

Tiger

Continent:	Asia
Habitat:	Rain forests, grasslands, savannas and even mangrove swamps
Life Span:	**Male**: 8-10 years **Female**: 12-15 years
Height:	80 – 110 cm
Weight:	**Male**: 90-310 kg **Female**: 65-170 kg
Food Type:	Carnivore
Active Time:	Most active at night
Conservation Status:	**Endangered**
Other:	60-65 km/h

Tigers are big, tigers are strong,
They're often in the forests where they belong.
Their stripes are orange and black,
Their roar can make you jump back.

They like to hunt and to stalk,
But they're also happy just to walk.
They have sharp claws and long teeth,
And they sometimes climb up trees.

Tigers have keen eyes to see ,
In the night they find prey with ease.
They live around the world, we try to preserve,
And they're endangered so this needs to be heard.

Let's help to protect them and keep them safe,
So that tigers can survive and thrive in their place.

Elephant

Continent:	Africa and Asia
Habitat:	Savannas, grasslands, and forests but occupy a wide range of habitats, including deserts, swamps, and highlands in tropical and subtropical regions of Africa and Asia
Life Span:	**Asian:** 48 years **African:** 60-70 years
Height:	**Asian:** 2.8 m **African:** 3.2 m
Weight:	**Asian:** 4000 kg **African:** 6000 kg
Food Type:	Herbivores
Active Time:	Crepuscular—they typically sleep during the day and are most active at dawn and dusk
Conservation Status:	**Endangered** and **Critically Endangered** (African forest elephant)
Other:	Speed: 40 km/h

Elephants are the biggest land animals you'll see,
They can be found in forests and savannahs so green.

Their trunks are so strong, they can reach high and low,
And with them they can carry things you'd never know.

Their ears are so big, they flap in the breeze,
Helping them cool off with ease.

Their tusks are so long, they're used for digging and more,
To break open tough logs and new treats to explore.

They have a deep bond with their family and friends,
With them they have fun and play 'till the day ends.

So, if you ever spot an elephant in the wild,
Stand and admire, but to them be kind.

Giraffe

Continent:	Africa
Habitat:	Semi-arid savannah and savannah woodlands
Life Span:	25 years
Height:	**Male**: 5-5.9 m **Female**: 4.3-5.2 m
Weight:	**Male**: 800-1900 kg **Female**: 550-1200 kg
Food Type:	Herbivores
Active Time:	Most active in the early morning and late afternoon but also feed at night in bright moonlight
Conservation Status:	**Endangered** and **Critically Endangered**
Other:	Giraffes are the tallest mammals on Earth

Once upon a time in Africa, far from the sea,
Lived a giraffe with a long neck as tall as a tree.
She had spots all over, from head to toe,
It was quite the sight to behold.

Her tongue was long, and her eyes were bright,
She munched on leaves both day and night.
The acacia tree was her favourite treat,
Which she ate on her four-toed feet.

The African sun shined down on her head,
As she roamed in search of food to be fed.
Her neck swayed back and forth as she walked,
 A view from height, so she was never stalked.

Giraffes are gentle creatures you see,
And they live in herds of up to twenty-three.
In Africa they roam around,
Always looking for something to be found.

Zebra

Continent:	Africa
Habitat:	Treeless grasslands and savanna woodlands
Life Span:	20 years
Height:	1.2 to 1.5 m
Weight:	280-400 kg
Food Type:	Herbivores
Active Time:	Most active during daylight.
Conservation Status:	Near threatened
Other:	Speed: 65 km/h

The zebra is a symbol of Africa's pride,
A majestic creature that cannot be denied.
It roams the savannah, from east to west,
A beautiful sight that's hard to forget.

Its stripes are special, and no two the same,
A pattern of beauty, that deserves fame.
Its stripes help protect from predators around,
By blending in with the grassy ground.

They roam the grassy plains,
In search of food and water to sustain.
With their powerful hooves they gallop and prance,
A sight to behold and worth a second glance.

Their diet consists of grass and leaves,
They need a lot to stay alive.
So, when you see them in the wild,
Remember to stay low and hide.

Gorilla

Continent:	Africa
Habitat:	From open plains to thick brush and dry thorn forest.
Life Span:	**Male**: 8-10 years **Female**: 15-16 years
Height:	**Male**: 1.2 m **Female**: 90-110 cm
Weight:	**Male**: 190 kg **Female**: 130 kg
Food Type:	Carnivore
Active Time:	Most active during the day.
Conservation Status:	**Endangered**
Other:	We share around 98% of our DNA with gorillas!

Gorillas are so awesome, their behaviour is quite calm,
But their roar is remarkable, like a sounding alarm.
They live in the African jungle, where there's lots of trees,
So look up to see, gorillas swinging in the leaves.

Gorillas have families that stay close and strong,
The silverback protects them, he's been there all along.
Gorillas are amazing creatures, they're gentle and kind,
Learning more about them is something you should find.

In the jungle they live, mostly in groups,
Communicating with, hoots and whoops.
They eat mostly fruits and leaves each day,
And sometimes insects too along the way.

Let's all work together, hand in hand,
To protect these gentle giants and their land.
Let's make sure their future is bright,
And their numbers increase without might.

Hippopotamus

Continent:	Africa
Habitat:	Slow-moving rivers and lakes
Life Span:	40 – 50 years
Height:	1.3 – 1.6 m
Weight:	**Male**: 1500-1800 kg **Female**: 1300-1500 kg
Food Type:	Primarily herbivorous, been observed to engage in omnivorous behavior.
Active Time:	Most active at night
Conservation Status:	Vulnerable
Other:	Hippos can't actually swim!

Hippos are so large and grey,
It's hard to believe they can float and play.
They live in rivers and lakes,
In the mud they sleep and shake.

In the land of Africa, they make their home,
Where they spend the night, never alone.
They stay cool by taking a dip,
In the water they splash away with a flip!

Their skin is thick like armour of steel,
So, no one dares come close, for the danger is real.
Hippos can sprout up to four feet tall,
And their weight goes up to two tons overall!

But let us remember while we play,
That hippos need our help today!

Cheetah

Continent:	Africa
Habitat:	Shrublands, grasslands, savannahs, and temperate to hot deserts
Life Span:	8-10 years
Height:	67 – 94 cm
Weight:	21-72 kg
Food Type:	Carnivore
Active Time:	Hunt mostly at night and rest during the day, often active at dawn and dusk and on cooler days.
Conservation Status:	Vulnerable
Other:	Speed: 80 – 130 km/h

A creature fast and wild,
the cheetah, is the fastest child.
It has black spots, on golden brown,
that swirl across its fur like a crown.

His claws are sharp, his eyes are keen,
To catch his prey, he must be mean.
But when he's not hunting for food,
This majestic animal is really quite good!

It has long legs and a slender frame,
Its tail helps it balance when it trains.
It hunts during the day and rests at night,
But its prey must always be in sight.

It lives in Africa and Asia too,
so, make sure to look for clues.
If you spot one out in the sun,
snap a picture for an amazing run!

Kangaroo

Continent:	Australia
Habitat:	Forests, woodlands, plains, and savannas
Life Span:	8-12 years
Height:	0.8-2 m
Weight:	40-66 kg
Food Type:	Herbivores
Active Time:	Dawn and dusk
Conservation Status:	Not endangered
Other:	They can hop 8 metres in a single bound!

Kangaroos like to hop around,
Their legs so strong and so sound.
Leaping and bounding through the trees,
Their bodies so fast with such ease.

In the wild they can be found,
Their pouch so large with little bound.
Keeping their young safe and secure,
Away from danger they ensure.

Their movements are unique and so quick,
They can travel over land so thick.
Their muscles are strong and so lean,
They can even jump over a fence, clean.

Their lives in the wild is so vast,
With the sun shining, their days are never aghast.
With this poem I hope you all now know,
The kangaroo is a fascinating animal to show.

Polar Bear

Continent:	North America, Europe, and Asia
Habitat:	Arctic sea ice
Life Span:	20-30 years
Height:	**Male**: 2.4-3 m **Female**: 1.8-2.4 m
Weight:	**Male**: 450 kg **Female**: 150-250 kg
Food Type:	Carnivore
Active Time:	Most active in the first third of the day and least active the final third of the day
Conservation Status:	Vulnerable
Other:	A polar bear skin is actually black

Polar bears so big and white,
Living in the cold and icy night.
They live on the floating sea ice,
Where they hunt for their favourite treats.

Their coats keep them warm day and night,
It's like a parka made just right.
Their fur is white to help them hide,
Making it hard to spot them outside.

They are strong swimmers of the north,
Swimming through icy waters forth.
But melting ice brings them much strife,
It messes with their way of life.

So, let's take care of our planet Earth,
Protecting all polar bears since birth!

Fox

Continent:	Every continent except Antarctica
Habitat:	Urban & gardens, rivers and wetland, coastal & marshland, deciduous woodland, mixed woodland, arable land.
Life Span:	3-4 years
Height:	35-50 cm
Weight:	2.2 – 14 kg
Food Type:	Omnivore
Active Time:	Dawn or dusk
Conservation Status:	Least Concern
Other:	Foxes can make over 40 different sounds

Funny little foxes, they live in their den,
They hunt in the night, so sometimes at ten.
Their fur is so soft, and their tails are so fluffy,
Their eyes are so sharp, the see when you look scruffy.

At night when you're sleeping, look out your window,
You might just catch a glimpse of a fox on the go.
He'll scurry about, his nose close to the ground,
And he'll soon find his dinner, the hunt has been found!

Foxes live in families, with their moms and their dads,
They take care of each other, and it makes them so glad.
They sing and they play, and they like to explore,
And with each other they build a bond that is pure.

Foxes love to run fast, and they can jump high too,
They're very clever creatures, there's no doubt that's true.
So next time you spot one, why not stop and watch,
These little furry critters are sure top-notch!

Wolf

Continent:	Eurasia and North America.
Habitat:	Temperate forests, mountains, tundra, taiga, grasslands and deserts.
Life Span:	14 years
Height:	80 – 85 cm
Weight:	**Male**: 30-80 kg **Female**: 23-55 kg
Food Type:	Carnivore
Active Time:	Dawn and dusk
Conservation Status:	Least Concern
Other:	Wolves hunt in packs

Wolves are creatures that make a howl,
Their fur is thick and they're quite proud.
Their pack is large, and they stay together,
In search of food in any weather.

They can be found in the forest or a plain,
And you may even hear them cry out in the rain.
Across miles of land their howl can extend,
It's a call to the pack and a message they send.

Wolves are quite brave, and they work in teams,
Leading each other to food and streams.
They hunt for their food like deer or moose,
And the prey is never left without a good ruse.

So, remember that wolves are strong and brave,
And their pack will always have their place.
Let us appreciate these animals wild,
For their loyalty and courage will never grow mild.

Alligator

Continent:	North America and Asia
Habitat:	Freshwater, slow-moving rivers, swamps, marshes and lakes
Life Span:	30-50 years
Length:	**Male**: 3.4 m **Female**: 2.6 m
Weight:	**Male**: 230 kg **Female**: 91 kg
Food Type:	Carnivore
Active Time:	Dawn and dusk
Conservation Status:	Least Concern
Other:	Their eyes glow in the dark

Alligators stay in the swamp,
Living in a damp and dank romp.
Their tails are long and their teeth so sharp,
They make a loud noise when they need to fart.

Their eyes are small, and their skin is green,
But don't be fooled by what you've seen.
For alligators can be quite sly,
And they can move faster than the blink of an eye.

He spends most of his day in the sun,
On land or in water, his days are fun.
His favorite food is fish, frogs, and birds,
He also likes turtles and small rodents.

He can grow up to ten feet long,
His presence is powerful so strong.
He's an apex predator, at the top of the food chain,
He is an amazing creature, it's no wonder he reigns!

Snake - Boa Constrictor

Continent:	South America
Habitat:	Deserts, wet tropical forests, open savannas and cultivated fields.
Life Span:	25 to 30 year
Length:	**Male**: 1.8-2.4 m **Female**: 2.1-3 m
Weight:	27 kg
Food Type:	Carnivore
Active Time:	Hunt mostly at night and rest during the day, often active at dawn and dusk and on cooler days.
Conservation Status:	**Endangered**
Other:	After a large meal, a boa doesn't need to eat again for weeks!

Snakes slither and hiss,
They make a noise like this.
Though they look scary and brave,
Most of them are quite afraid.

Snakes mostly live in warm, dry places,
Like deserts and jungles, with plenty of spaces.
Some can be found in water and trees,
Sometimes camouflaged so you can't see.

Snakes can smell with their tongues,
They can tell when danger is close among.
Their eyes are small and round,
Their colors can be found in different hues all around.

But don't be scared if you see one come,
They would rather run than fight and hurt someone.
We should respect them for the important job they do,
Helping to keep a balance in nature for me and you!

Sea turtle

Continent:	Every continent except Antarctica
Habitat:	Most of the world's oceans, apart from cold polar seas.
Life Span:	30-50 years
Length:	83 – 114 cm
Weight:	300 – 500 kg
Food Type:	Herbivores
Active Time:	Primarily diurnal
Conservation Status:	**Endangered**
Other:	They can hold their breath for five hours underwater !

Turtles so slow, but quite wise it seems,
Their shells come in many colours and gleams.
From the beach to the lake, they can be found,
No matter the place, their stories abound.

They spend much of their time below the waves,
Trying to find something to eat or plays.
Their flippers help them swim with ease,
And they can dive down deep into the seas.

They can live in water and on land,
Their habitats are both so grand.
Bright eyes watch all around them,
So sometimes they'll hide in a den.

So, let's all work together to save our seas,
And protect these creatures for centuries.
Let's keep our oceans clean and safe,
For turtles to live in peace and grace.

Macaw Parrot

Continent:	Central America, North America (only Mexico), South America
Habitat:	Rainforests, woodland
Life Span:	35 to 50 years
Height:	30-102 cm
Weight:	1-1.7 kg
Food Type:	Omnivores
Active Time:	Dawn and dusk
Conservation Status:	Least Concern (Population decreasing)
Other:	Macaws fall in love and stay that way !

Parrots are so fun and colourful too,
Their beaks and feathers, what a view.
They can copy the words that you say,
But might not remember the next day.

They can fly high with no fear,
Through the sky above so clear.
These colourful birds are quite smart,
They can learn tricks that are a work of art.

Parrots make nice pets to keep,
Caring for them is not too steep.
A cage and food and lots of fun,
You'll have a best friend when you're done!

Parrots can teach us a thing or two,
Like never give up, you can do it too.
Their intelligence is something to see,
So let's learn from parrots and respect their family.

Koala Bear

Continent:	Australia
Habitat:	Coastal islands and tall eucalypt forests to low inland woodlands
Life Span:	13 – 18 years
Height:	60–85 cm
Weight:	4 – 15 kg
Food Type:	Herbivore
Active Time:	Most active in the morning
Conservation Status:	**Endangered**
Other:	May sleep for 18 to 22 hours!

Twinkle twinkle little koala,
In the trees so high you go,
You live in Australia, down below.
Eucalyptus leaves you do eat,
They give you energy just like meat.

You sleep and nap during the day,
And share with us your fuzzy grey.
Your cute face and round ears so furry,
So cuddly, so lovable and rarely in a hurry.

Your coat is thick and helps protect,
From the cold and heat, no need to fret.
At night you wander the forest floor,
Searching for food, it's such a chore.

We can plant more trees for them to live in,
And keep their habitats safe and sound.
So they can stay happy and healthy within,
And never have to leave their ground.

Rhinoceros

Continent:	Africa, Asia
Habitat:	Roam grassland and open savannah.
Life Span:	35-50 years
Height:	1.3 – 1.9 m
Weight:	700 – 3500 kg
Food Type:	Herbivores
Active Time:	Most active at night
Conservation Status:	**Critically Endangered**
Other:	The name rhinoceros means 'nose horn'

Rhinoceros, so big and strong,
With their horns so sharp and long.
Their thick skin like armor so tough,
They roam in Africa where it's hot enough.

It spends its days walking and grazing,
On plants and grass that it's been tasting.
It's a strong animal with a powerful build,
And an appetite that never gets filled.

Rhinoceroses are herbivores,
Feeding on grass and leaves galore.
They often live alone, it's what they prefer,
Protecting them is what we must do for sure.

This amazing creature needs our help,
To keep it safe from harm and yelp.
So let's work together to ensure its safety,
And ensure that rhino populations stay healthy!

Hyena

Continent:	Africa
Habitat:	Savannas, grasslands, woodlands, forest edges, subdeserts, and even mountains
Life Span:	12-20 years
Height:	60-92 cm
Weight:	**Male**: 40-55kg **Female**: 44-64kg
Food Type:	Primarily carnivore
Active Time:	Generally nocturnal
Conservation Status:	Least Concern (Population decreasing)
Other:	The hyena is more closely related to the mongoose and cat than the dog !

A hyena is an animal quite sly,
With teeth that are sharp and a laugh that is high.
Their spots are like polka dots, that's all they need,
To help them blend in, with the tall grass and reed.

Their jaws are powerful, their teeth sharp and strong,
They can crack bones, all night long.
Their diet is varied, they'll eat what they can scope,
From insects to birds, to the odd antelope.

Their laugh is most distinctive, it's loud and clear,
Hyena laughter can be heard from far and near.
Known to be scavengers, but they'll do more than that.
They hunt small prey, like birds and rats.

Hyenas are fierce and not scared of much,
Though the lion is king, hyenas won't hush.
So if you see one in the wild, don't be too bold,
And be sure to keep your distance from this fellow!

Emu

Continent:	Australia
Habitat:	Open arid plains, tropical woodlands
Life Span:	25 to 28 years
Height:	1.5-2 m
Weight:	**Male**: 32kg **Female**: 37kg
Food Type:	Primarily herbivore
Active Time:	Most active during the day
Conservation Status:	Least Concern (Population stable)
Other:	Speed: 50 km/h

An Emu is tall and can't fly,
Its feathers are soft but its legs are spry,
The Emu is large it can't be denied,
It loves a good meal and a place to hide.

It lives in the Outback of Australia's land,
It's a flightless bird but this was planned.
It will outrun you with its powerful stride,
Its feathers are brown with a hint of blue on the side.

Its legs are strong and long,
Perfect for running along.
If you ever see one on the move,
You'd be astonished at how quickly it can groove.

So now you've heard everything about an Emu,
A unique bird that lives down under too.
He's friendly and gentle and quite a sight to see,
So, remember him each time you say "G 'day matey"!

Printed in Great Britain
by Amazon

14211854R00027